JAZZ FAVORITES

ISBN 978-1-4234-2152-8

HAL•LEONARD®
CORPORATION

7777 W. BLUEMOUND RD. P.O. BOX 13819 MILWAUKEE, WI 53213

Visit Hal Leonard Online at
www.halleonard.com

All the Things You Are

from VERY WARM FOR MAY
Lyrics by Oscar Hammerstein II
Music by Jerome Kern

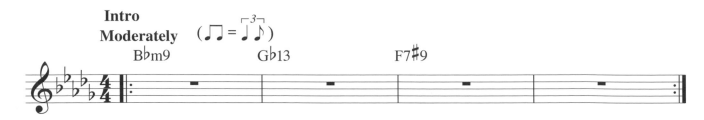

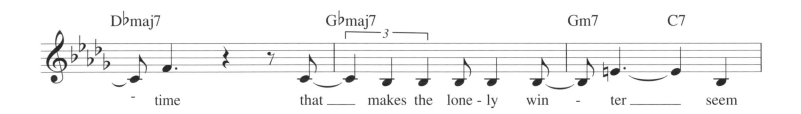

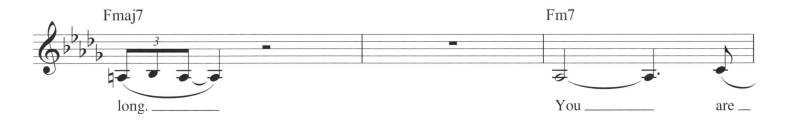

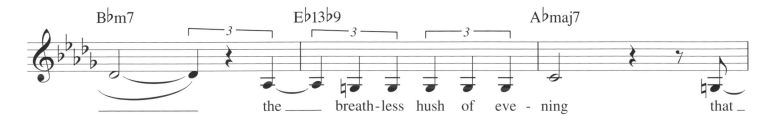

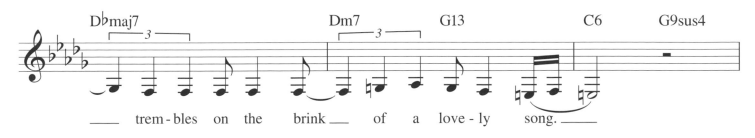

4

Blame It on My Youth

Words by Edward Heyman
Music by Oscar Levant

Intro
Slow Ballad

Verse

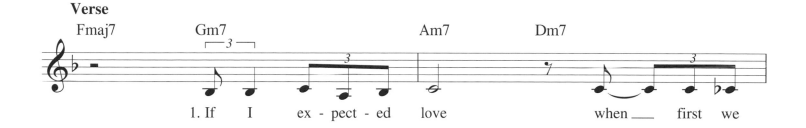

1. If I ex-pect-ed love when ___ first we

kissed, blame it on my youth.

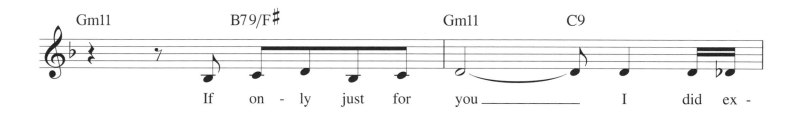

If on-ly just for you ___ I did ex-

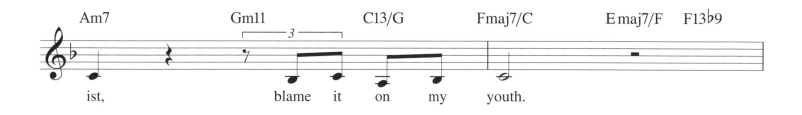

ist, blame it on my youth.

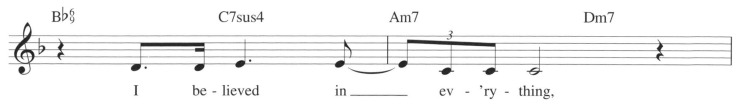

I be-lieved in ___ ev-'ry-thing,

first I learned __ the truth, don't blame it on my

heart, blame __ it on my youth. __

Instrumental

Verse

3. And if I cried _____ a lit-tle bit _____ when

first I learned _____ the truth,

don't blame it on my heart, blame __ it on __

__ my __ youth. _____

Bésame Mucho
(Kiss Me Much)

Music and Spanish Words by Consuelo Velazquez
English Words by Sunny Skylar

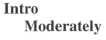

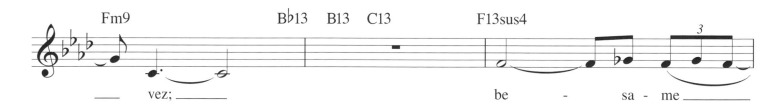

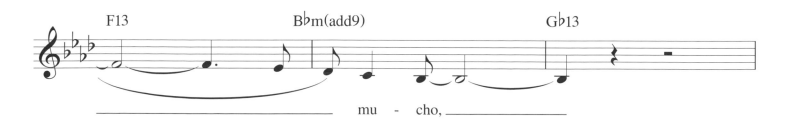

Fm(add9)   Db7   C7   Fm7   Bb13

que ten - go mie - do   per - der - te, ___ per - der - te ___ des pues. _____

Instrumental

B13   C13   Fm$_9^6$ F7$_{\#5}^{\#9}$ Bbm9

Ab13sus4   Gm11b5   C7#9   C75#9   Fm9   Bb13

B13   C13   C7#9   Cm(add9)/F   F7$_{\#5}^{\#9}$ Bbm9

Gb13   Fm$_9^6$ Db7   C7   Fm$_9^6$ Bb13

Bridge

B13   C13   Gm11   C7   Fm7   Bb7

Quie - ro te - ner - te muy cer - ca,   mi - rar me en

Bm/D   C7   Fm7   Fm6   Gm11   C7

tus o - jos, ver - te jun - to a mi, _____ pien - sa que tal vez

Fm7   Bb9   G7$_{\#5}^{\#9}$ C7sus4   C7b9

ma - na - na   yo ya es - ta - re le - jos,   muy le - jos de ti. ___

By Myself

from BETWEEN THE DEVIL

Words by Howard Dietz
Music by Arthur Schwartz

Intro
Brightly

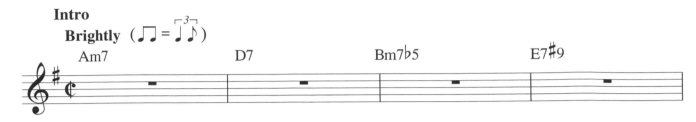

1. I'll go _____ my way by my - self.
2. *Instrumental*

Here's where the com - e - dy _____ ends. _____

I'll have _____

_____ to de - ny _____ my - self

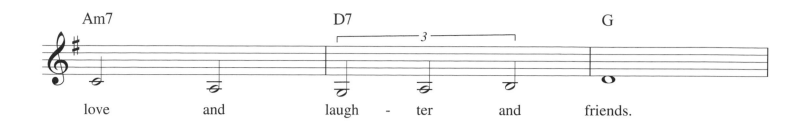

Am7   D7   G

love   and   laugh - ter   and   friends.

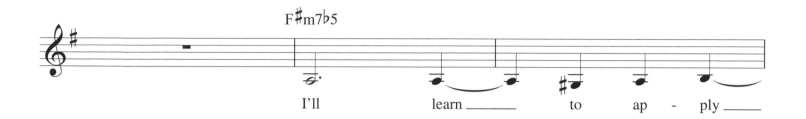

F#m7♭5

I'll   learn _____ to   ap - ply _____

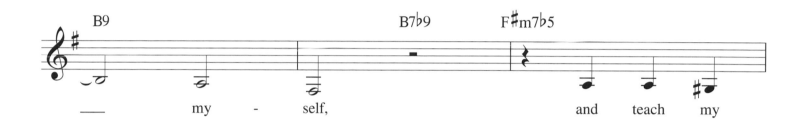

B9   B7♭9   F#m7♭5

___   my - self,   and   teach   my

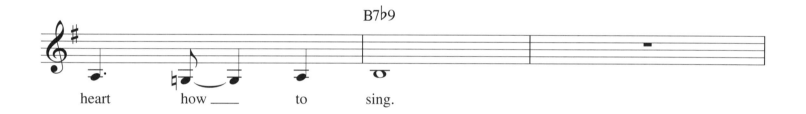

B7♭9

heart   how ___ to   sing.

G7sus4   G7♭9   C6/9

I'll   go _____ my   way   by   my -   self, _

F13#11   Am7   D13♭9

___   like   a   bird   on ___ a

To Coda ⊕

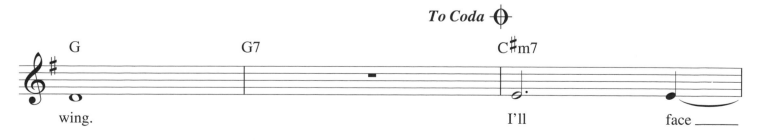

G   G7   C#m7

wing.   I'll   face ___

the un - known,

I'll build a world of ___ my own, _____

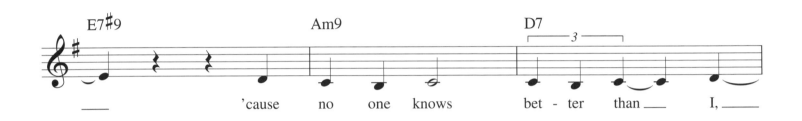

___ 'cause no one knows bet - ter than ___ I, _____

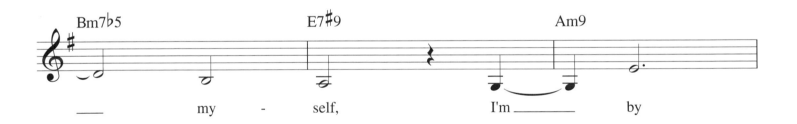

___ my - self, I'm _____ by

D.S. al Coda

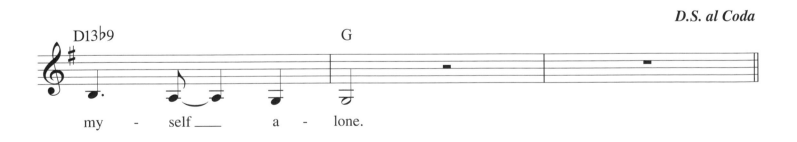

my - self ___ a - lone.

Coda

I'll face _____ the un - known, _____

Bm7♭5

I'll build a world all

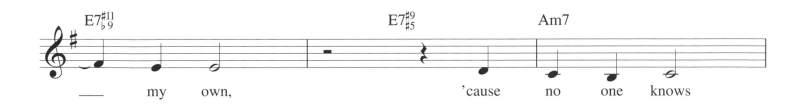

E7♯11♭9   E7♯9♯5   Am7

my own, 'cause no one knows

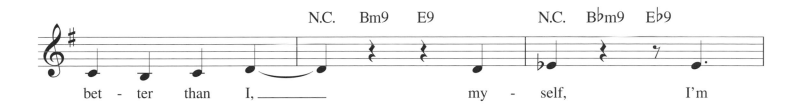

N.C. Bm9 E9 N.C. B♭m9 E♭9

bet - ter than I, my - self, I'm

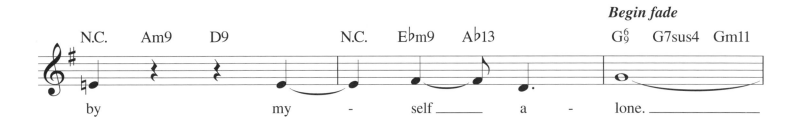

N.C. Am9 D9 N.C. E♭m9 A♭13 *Begin fade* G⁶₉ G7sus4 Gm11

by my - self a - lone.

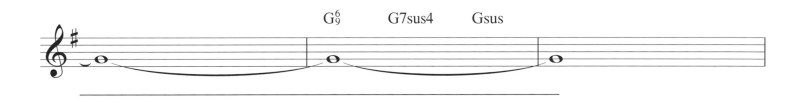

G⁶₉ G7sus4 Gsus

G⁶₉ G7sus4 Gm11 G⁶₉ G7sus4 Gsus

Repeat and fade

G⁶₉ G7sus4 Gm11

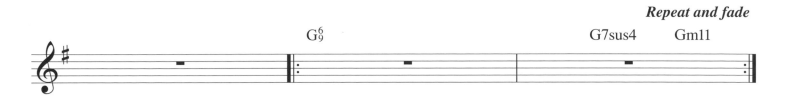

The Lady Is a Tramp

from BABES IN ARMS
from WORDS AND MUSIC

Words by Lorenz Hart
Music by Richard Rodgers

Intro
Bright Latin

Verse

1. I ___ get too ___ hun - gry ___ for din - ner at

eight. I ___ like the the - a - tre,

but nev - er come late. I _____

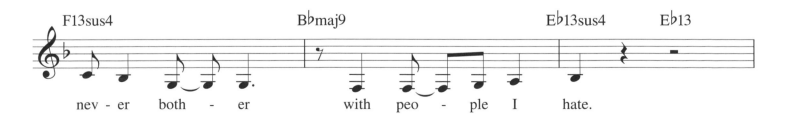

nev - er both - er with peo - ple I hate.

life with-out care. ____ I'm broke,

Verse

'at's oke. ___ 3. Hate Cal - i - for - nia, it's

cold and it's damp. That's why the la -

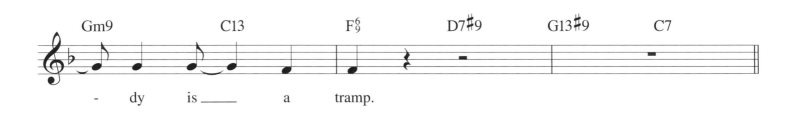

- dy is ___ a tramp.

Interlude

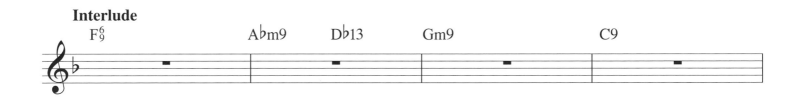

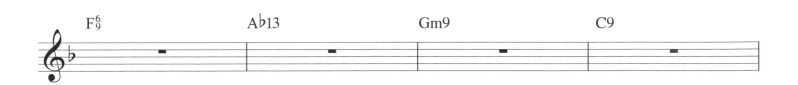

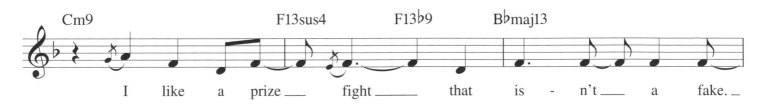

I like a prize ___ fight ___ that is - n't ___ a fake. ___

_ That's why the la - dy is a

tramp.

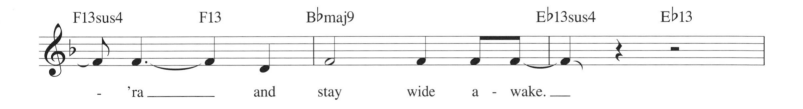

I go to op -

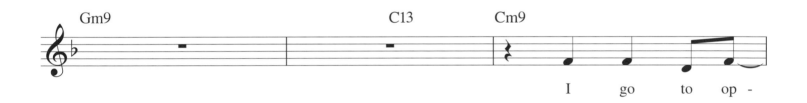

- 'ra _____ and stay wide a - wake. __

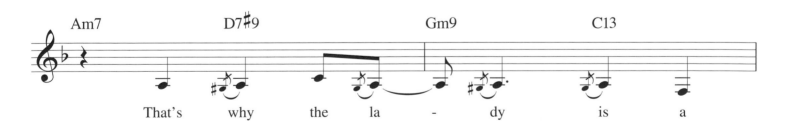

That's why the la - dy is a

Bridge

tramp. I ____ like the green grass _

un - der my shoes.

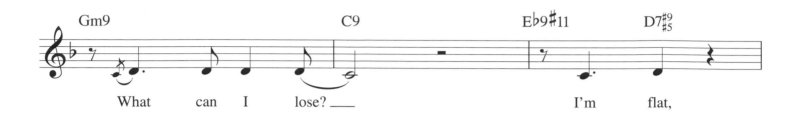

What can I lose? ___ I'm flat,

Outro-Verse

'at's that. ___ 4. I'm ___ all a - lone ___ when I

low - er my ___ lamp. ___ That's why the la -

- dy is, ___ that's why they call the la - dy,

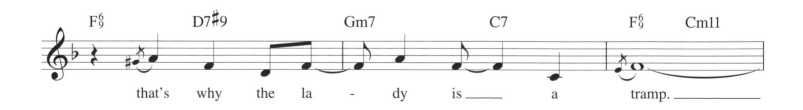

that's why the la - dy is ___ a tramp. ___

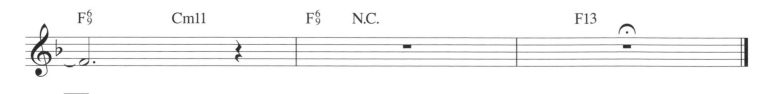

On a Clear Day
(You Can See Forever)

from ON A CLEAR DAY YOU CAN SEE FOREVER

Words by Alan Jay Lerner
Music by Burton Lane

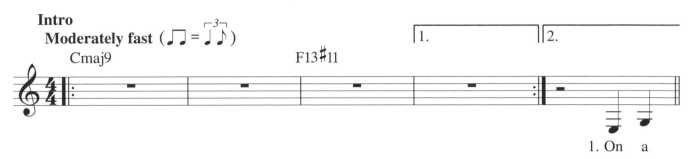

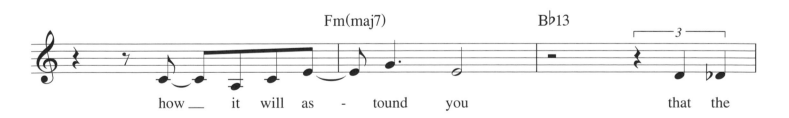

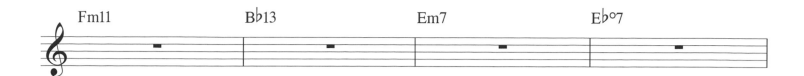

Fm11　　　　　Bb13　　　　　Em7　　　　　Eb°7

Dm9　　　　　　　　　　　　**Bridge**
　　　　　　　　　　　　　　G13　　Gm9

You ___ feel ___ part of ___

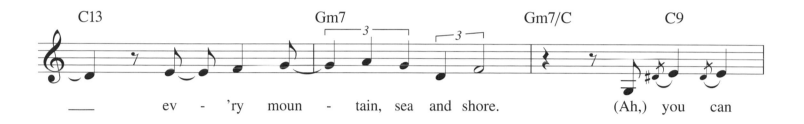

C13　　　　　Gm7　　　　　Gm7/C　　C9

___ ev - 'ry moun - tain, sea and shore. (Ah,) you can

F⁶₉　　　　　D13　　　　　Dm7　　A7b9

hear, from far and ___ near, ___ a world you nev - er heard be - fore.

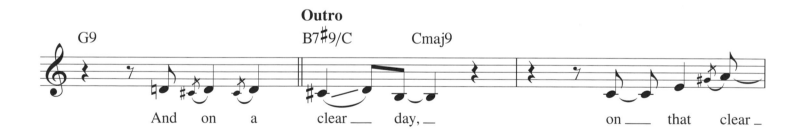

Outro
G9　　　　　B7#9/C　　Cmaj9

And on a clear ___ day, ___ on ___ that clear ___

Em9　　　　　A7b9　　　　　Dm7　　Em7

___ day, ___ you can see for -

Repeat and fade

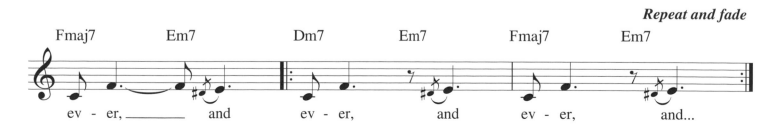

Fmaj7　Em7　　　Dm7　　Em7　　　Fmaj7　Em7

ev - er, ___ and ev - er, and ev - er, and...

Love Letters

Theme from the Paramount Picture LOVE LETTERS

Words by Edward Heyman
Music by Victor Young

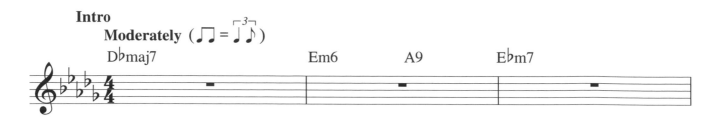

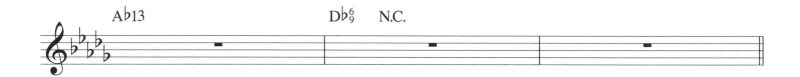

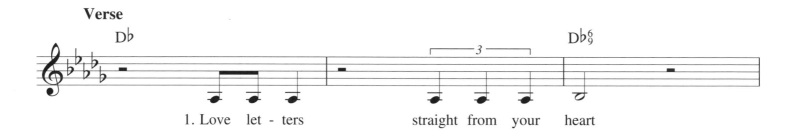

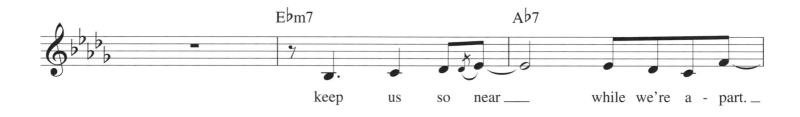

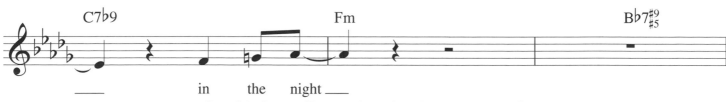

Ebm9 ... Bb7

when I know that I have all the love __

Ebm7 ... Ab7#9 ... **Verse** Db6/9

_____ you write. __ 2. I mem - o - rize __

__ ev - 'ry line, __

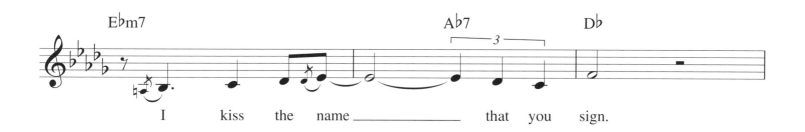

Ebm7 ... Ab7 ... Db

I kiss the name _____ that you sign.

Db7 ... Gbmaj7 ... Ebm11b5

Then I re - call __ once __ a - gain

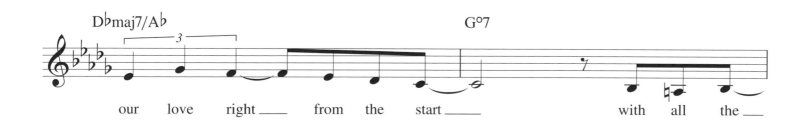

Dbmaj7/Ab ... G°7

our love right __ from the start __ with all the __

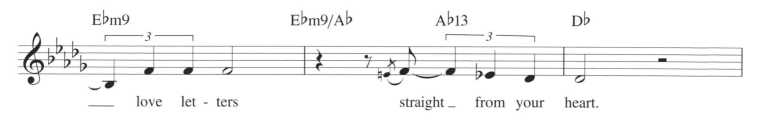

Ebm9 ... Ebm9/Ab ... Ab13 ... Db

__ love let - ters straight __ from your heart.

Instrumental

Ebm7   Ab7   Db

Ebm7   Ab7

Db$^{6}_{9}$ Gm11b5   Db7#9 C7#9

Fm(add9)   B7#5   Ebm9   B7 Bb7

Verse

Ebm11   Ab7#5   Db6

2. I _____ mem - o - rize _____

Db$^{6}_{9}$

_____ ev - 'ry sin - gle line, _____

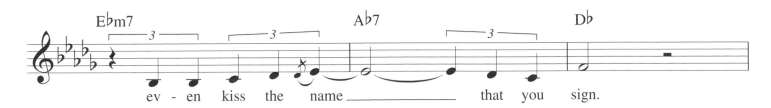

Ebm7   Ab7   Db

ev - en kiss the name _____ that you sign.

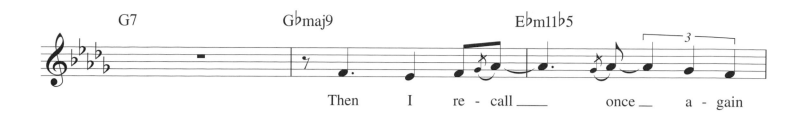

Then I re-call ____ once ____ a - gain

our love right ____ from the start ____ with all the ____ love let - ters

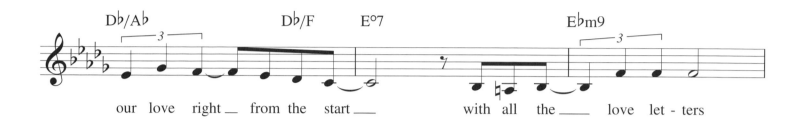

straight ____ from your heart, with all ____ the

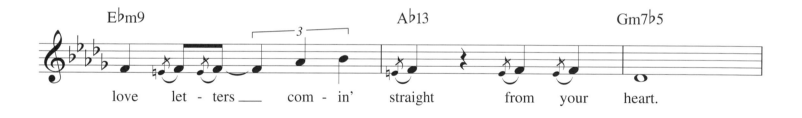

love let - ters ____ com - in' straight from your heart.

Sentimental Journey

Words and Music by Bud Green, Les Brown and Ben Homer

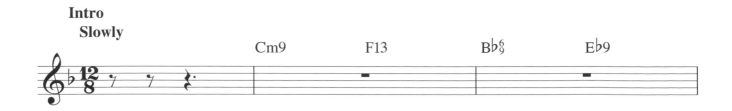

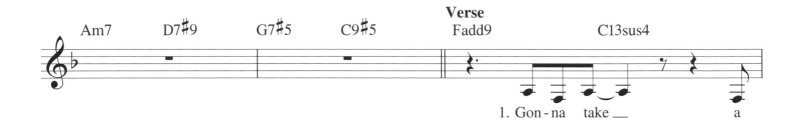

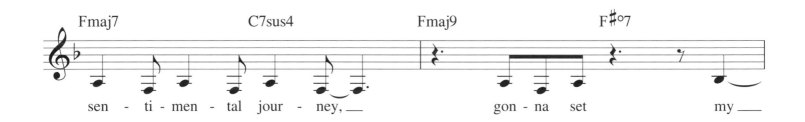

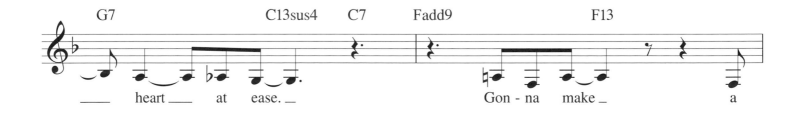

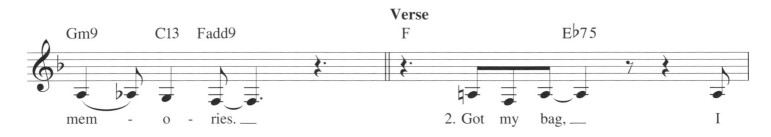

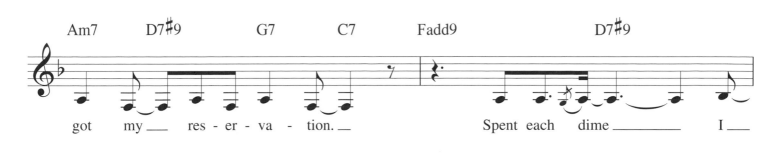

Am7   D7#9   G7   C7   Fadd9   D7#9

got my ___ res - er - va - tion. ___ Spent each dime _____ I ___

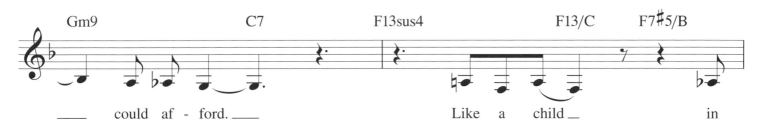

Gm9   C7   F13sus4   F13/C   F7#5/B

___ could af - ford. ___ Like a child ___ in

Bb9   Eb13   Fmaj7   D79

wild an - ti - ci - pa - tion, ___ long ___ to hear that ___

Bridge

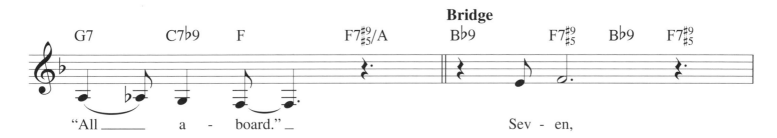

G7   C7b9   F   F7#9#5/A   Bb9   F7#9#5   Bb9   F7#9#5

"All _____ a - board." ___ Sev - en,

B9/C   Bo7   F6/9   Bb13

that's the ___ time _ we leave. ___ At ___ sev - en, ___

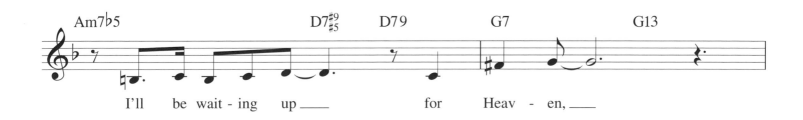

Am7b5   D7#9#5   D79   G7   G13

I'll be wait - ing up ___ for Heav - en, ___

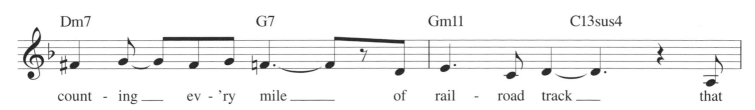

Dm7   G7   Gm11   C13sus4

count - ing ___ ev - 'ry mile _____ of rail - road track ___ that

Verse

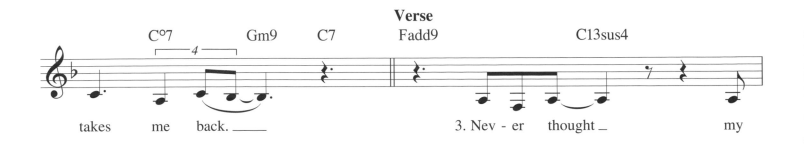

takes   me   back. _____   3. Nev - er   thought _   my

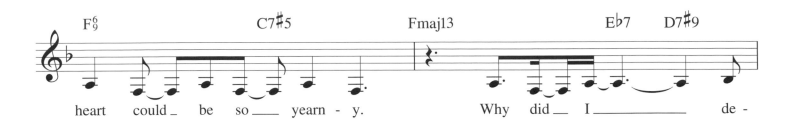

heart   could _   be   so ____   yearn - y.   Why   did _   I _____   de -

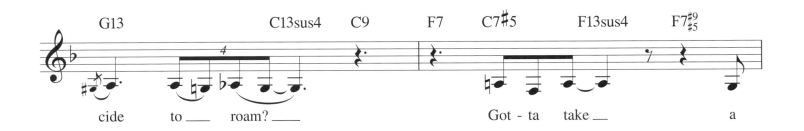

cide   to ____   roam? ____   Got - ta   take _   a

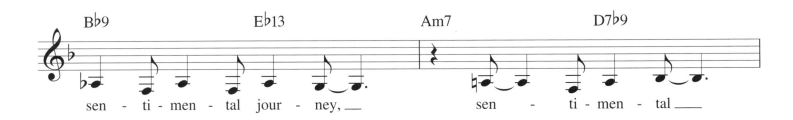

sen - ti - men - tal   jour - ney, _   sen - ti - men - tal ____

Interlude

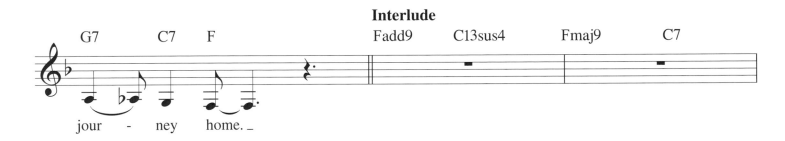

jour - ney   home. _

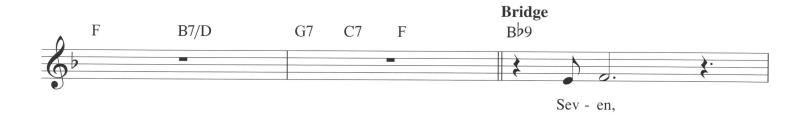

Sev - en,

that's the time we leave. ____ At ____ sev - en, ____

I'll be wait - ing up ____ for ____ Heav - en.

Count - in' ev - 'ry mile ____ of rail - road track ____ that

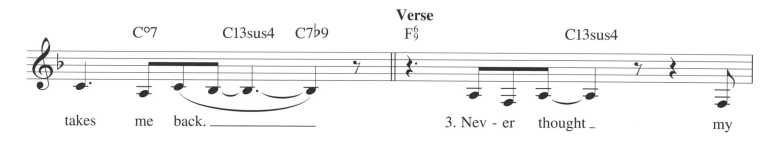

takes me back. ____ 3. Nev - er thought ____ my